DISCOVER THE ISLE OF GIGHA

KEITH T. WILSON

ISBN: 978-1-5272-6270-6

First published in 2020 by
eilean publishing.
Heather Lea, Isle of Gigha,
Argyll and Bute, PA41 7AA,
Scotland.

Printed in the U.K. by

the smart way to print

- For Marion -
x

Special thanks to:

John Bannatyne
Catherine Czerkawska
Gigha Coast and Countryside Group
John Martin

On the Cover: Queen's beach and Bàgh na Dòirlinn next to Eilean Garbh in the north. See page 28.

On the Title Page: Sea Pinks on the rocky shore at East Tarbert Bay. Original photo processed using an art filter.

On the Back Cover: Gigha heather in full bloom with the Paps of Jura visible in the far distance.

Contents

Introduction

THE ISLE OF GIGHA - A HEBRIDEAN ISLAND PARADISE

Photo: PA

The community-owned Isle of Gigha, pronounced "*geea*", is some 11km long, 2.5km wide and lies just 4.5km from the Kintyre peninsula, from which it is separated, by the Sound of Gigha. The 'Lochranza' car ferry runs on a regular daily basis from Tayinloan on the Kintyre mainland with the journey taking just twenty minutes.

Gigha has been occupied for around 5000 years and evidence of its former inhabitants can still be found today. The Vikings called it *Gudey* and King Håkon of Norway anchored his fleet here in 1263 before the Battle of Largs. The island is undulating and craggy with its west coast dominated by sea cliffs although its east coast is less precipitous. It has a mild climate with above average sunshine.

The island has a school, a village hall, a post office and shop, church, hotel, craft shops, cafe, activity centre, golf course seafood restaurant, airstrip and yacht moorings. It also has a number of B&Bs, self-catering lets, and a camp site.

For the visitor, there is a lots to see and do on Gigha which has a rich natural and historical heritage as well as beautiful white sands and glorious gardens of sub-tropical plants. No need to bring a car, just walk, cycle or sail to the 'wee isle'.

Gigha might be a small island but when you start to explore away from the road, it feels anything but small. Large areas are remote and in places inaccessible. Paths can be poor, with many being no more than cattle tracks. However the Isle of Gigha Heritage Trust have plans in place to undertake a major improvement of the path network. In winter, and after rainfall, wellington boots are essential for many of the locations listed and spring is a good time to explore the wilder parts of Gigha before the bracken and briars take over.

Please keep dogs on a lead near livestock, which can be encountered just about anywhere on the island. Also, shut gates and please don't leave any litter which might spoil this beautiful island. I hope you enjoy discovering all that the Isle of Gigha has to offer.

Each location in this guide has been graded based on difficulty.

 EASY: No special difficulties.

 FAIRLY EASY: Uneven ground, muddy paths, stile or fence to negotiate.

 MODERATE: Pathless sections, waterlogged ground, boulders/bracken/briars to negotiate, some ascent.

 HARDER: Location finding, tide requirements, steep drops close by.

Isle of
Gigha

Extract from
OS Landranger sheet 62
(North Kintyre and Tarbert)

|— 1 km —|

Map data

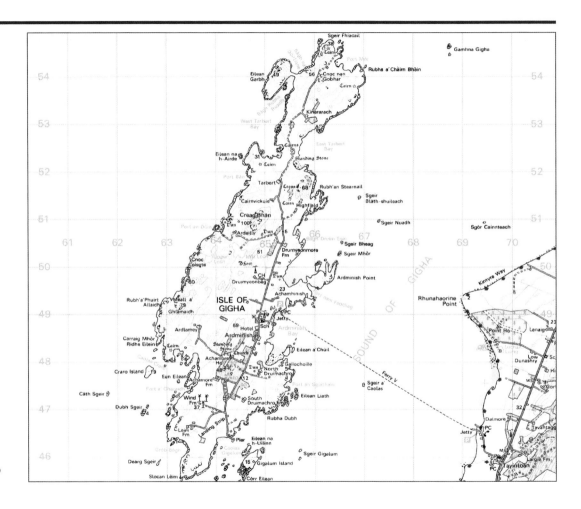

Sloc an Leim 'Spouting Cave'

OS Grid Reference: 6330 4563

The location

Between Port Mòr and Port Cùil is a mostly hidden narrow cleft through which seawater is forced. This is especially so at high tide in windy conditions. The water escapes from the cleft in a spout at its farthest point from the sea. Even in calm conditions you should be able to hear the rush of water as it journeys through the cleft. On the opposite side of the bay on top of a sea stack are the remains of Port Mòr Dun, an Iron Age fort. Further up the rocky coast towards Leim Beach you will find another narrow cleft in the rocks. This one is Sloc an Tranan, the 'Snoring Pit', named for the noise it makes in a storm. It also 'spouts' at times.

Getting there

From the south pier follow the coastline south west along the beaches and then a raised beach, keeping the old sea cliffs to your right. When you reach the old sea stack go through the gap between the cliff and the stack and this will lead you to Port Mòr - Sloc an Leim is on the far side. You can also reach the cave from the southern end of Leim Beach. Go over the stile, ascend the hill, and aim for the distant Càrn an Lèim (cairn). From here drop down to the south west to Port Mòr and the cave.

Right: 'Spouting Cave' can be accessed from the shore at a very low tide but be very wary!

Below: 'Snoring Pit' mostly 'rumbles' but at times can spout as well.

Above: The remains of Port Mòr Dun, an Iron Age fort, lie on the grassy top of this old sea stack. Debris from its walls can be seen in the foreground. Port Mòr is to the right in this photo.

Gròb Bàgh and Leim Beach

OS Grid Reference: 6339 4632

The location

A very picturesque location and one of the best beaches on Gigha, particularly on a calm sunny summer day when the waters of Gròb Bàgh look turquoise. The rocky outcrop just offshore gives the bay its name - 'Bay of the Point of Rock'. Just to the west of the prominent rocky outcrop is an exposed thick seam of pure white quartz which is best seen at low tide. If you walk further west along the beach and over the grassy shore you will reach the 'dark cliff', an ancient sea cliff composed of grey rock with lots of weathered cavities. A walk to the top will give you some great views towards Northern Ireland and Islay.

Getting there

Take the island road towards the south and take a right turn towards the wind turbines. After a few meters, head left at the junction. You will pass two houses on the right and the airfield on the left. When you reach the entrance to Leim Farm turn left along a track and through a farm gate. Follow the grassy track down the slope onto the beach.

Above: Looking down on Gròb Bàgh and Leim Beach from near the Leim Farm track.

Right: Stretching 150m from the beach out towards the sea is the Rubha Ban quartz vein. It is best seen at low tide when it is possible to walk all the way to the seaward end.

Below: The turquoise waters of Gròb Bàgh at Leim Beach.

Bodach and Cailleach standing stones

OS Grid Reference: 6382 4730

The location

Located on the rocky outcrop of Cnoc a' Shevis at Moinean Sitheil are two unusual ancient standing stones - Bodach, the old man and Cailleach, the old woman. The Bodach is flagon-shaped, curving in to a distinctive "neck" before broadening out to the "head" which has a narrow collar of quartz. The Cailleach is boat-shaped with a flat top. Visitors are often surprised just how small the standing stones are. Irish sailors had a high regard for the stones and would regularly visit leaving offerings at the site. It was believed that bad luck would descend on Gigha if the stones were to fall so locals and visitors always ensured the stones were righted promptly .

Getting there

Follow the island road south and turn right onto the track to the wind turbines. Keeping to the right, follow the track uphill. At the top go through the field gate on the right and cross the field past the wind turbine towards the rocky outcrop and ascend to the grassy top where you will find the stones. If you walk 100m NNW from the stones into the adjacent field you will find the remains of the Achamore Farm Neolithic chambered cairn.

Above: The odd-shaped and very ancient Bodach and Cailleach standing stones are to be found close to the 'dancing ladies' (wind turbines).

Left: The standing stones sit on the grassy top of a small rocky outcrop. They are very similar to those at Tigh nam Bodach in Glen Lyon, Perthshire.

Quern-stone Quarry

OS Grid Reference: 6330 4810

The location

Quern stones were used in the past for grinding grain and here on Gigha there are several locations in the south west where such stones were quarried. The quarry close to Port nan Cudainnean, 'Cuddyport', is perhaps the best example. Over a hundred quern stones were quarried from this location and then transported by boat. You can see the outlines of partially cut stones and the circular depressions where stones have been removed from the Amphibolite bedrock. Whilst here, it is worth visiting the lovely beach just to the west at Port an t-Samhlaidh, 'Bay of the Spectre'. From here you can walk around to the old stone pier and also follow a track up to the top of Meall an t-Samhlaidh, 'Hill of the Spectre', where you get fine views of distant Ireland.

Getting there

Follow the track uphill from the Achamore Gardens car park past the graveyard and at the junction before Ardlamey Farm turn left and follow the track and then the field edge to Cuddyport Cottage. Follow the track next to the cottage onto the shore and keep straight ahead along the small promontory where you will find the quarry on the west side.

Right: The rock used for the quern-stones here was not the best quality as it contains mica which can flake into flour and cause respiratory issues.

Below: The 'Bay of the Spectre' as seen from the track leading to the 'Hill of the Spectre'. The promontory containing the quern-stone quarry is near top centre.

Above: Low tide at Port an t-Samhlaidh. The 'Hill of the Spectre' is at far right above the old stone pier.

Kilchattan Chapel

OS Grid Reference: 6431 4809

The location

The chapel and graveyard were once part of an ancient religious site which had a holy well, cairns, a cross and a nearly 5m tall standing stone, none of which are now present. The old parish church is dedicated to St.Cathan, a contemporary

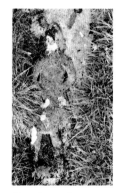

of St.Columba, and dates from the 13th century. The window in the east wall has a slab with two cupped-shaped depressions that could be a reused pagan altar. The font from the chapel is now located in Gigha Parish Church. The site has ten graves from the Middle Ages with beautiful carvings including swords, animals and plait work. Malcolm, the 15th century chieftain of Gigha, has his warrior likeness carved in high relief.

Getting there

Take the south road and turn right into the Achamore Gardens car park. Walk up the track past the village hall and you will reach the chapel and graveyard at the top of the hill on your right.

Above & below: The ruin of Kilchattan Chapel, 'The cell of St. Cathan'.

Far left: The grave of Chieftain Malcolm MacNeill 'of Geya'. He died in the year 1493.

Ogham standing stone

OS Grid Reference: 6426 4817

The location

Gigha's Ogham stone, a tall four-sided column, sits on Cnoc na Carraigh, 'Hill of the Pillar'. It was erected in early medieval times but is unlikely to be older than the 7th century and was erected in memory of a deceased leader. It features an ancient Irish linear script on its south west edge which is badly weathered and has sections missing due to damage caused to the stone. The stone has fallen twice but was re-erected close to its original site. The stone as you see it today is not complete, with a piece of the top being broken off in the mid 19th century and used elsewhere on the island. The Ogham script is either named after the Irish god Ogma, or after an Irish phrase which refers to the seam made by the point of a sharp weapon.

Getting there

Take the road south and turn right into Achamore Gardens car park. Walk up the track and keep right once past the graveyard. Just before you reach the Keil cottages go through the gate on the right and walk for a few metres along a path on the right to the stone which is hidden behind the gorse bushes.

Right: This rare 7th Century standing stone can be found on the lower slopes of Cnoc na Carraigh, 'Hill of the Pillar'.

Left: Various interpretations regarding the Ogham script present on the stone have been put forward. The experts are agreed that one of the scripts is 'maq' meaning 'son'. I am aware of several possible interpretations of the script including: Vicula, son of Cugini; Fiacal, son of Coemgen (Scottish); Viddosamo, son of Qoicogino (Pictish).

Due to weathering, damage and a covering of lichen and moss you will not be able to see the full inscription but if the light is just right you will see at least part of this ancient script.

Achamore Gardens

OS Grid Reference: 6420 4794

The location

Originally a sporting estate with mixed woodland for pheasant cover, the grounds of the 'Mansion House' were transformed beginning in 1944 by Colonel Sir James Horlick with the assistance of head gardener Malcolm Allan and garden designer Kitty Lloyd Jones. These beautiful gardens contain many notable plants from around the world including the renowned Horlick's rhododendron and camellia collections which flourish in Gigha's mild microclimate. The woodland walks with rhododendrons, azaleas, camellias, New Zealand tree ferns, hydrangeas and fuchsias and several notable and champion trees complement the walled garden with it's more tender specimens, herbaceous borders and a bamboo maze. Not to be missed is the viewpoint on the west side which has stunning views over to the islands of Islay and Jura. Look out for the peacocks which wander around the gardens.

Getting there

Take the road south and you will see the sign for the gardens at a junction on your right soon after leaving the village. Limited parking is available.

Above: The pond.

Right: Achamore House, the 'Mansion House', was built in 1884 by William James Scarlett. The privately owned house sits in a central position in the gardens.

Below: The walled garden

Uamh nan Calaman (cave)

OS Grid Reference: 6333 4949

The location

The impressive Uamh nan Calaman, 'Pigeons' Cave', lies on Gigha's west coast but visiting involves a steep descent to the rocky shore and then a scramble up a rocky slope to the cave. The cave is large and deep and you will probably find pigeons present which will fly past you. A torch is required to explore the deeper section of the cave. The cave is partially hidden from the shore by a rockfall at its entrance and so you only see the mouth of the cave properly once you get on top of the rockfall which is hidden under vegetation. It is possible to reach the cave from above but this route is not recommended due to the steepness of the slope.

Right: Looking out of 'Pigeon's Cave'. Part of the rockfall has tumbled into the cave and in wet conditions this can be very slippy.

Getting there

Go north past the shop and over the gate opposite the track to 'The Manse'. Head west around the gorse outcrops and then cross over a broken stile at an old wall. Continue west across the fields and when you reach the wilder vegetation look for a yellow-topped pole on a high spot. From here continue west keeping the big pond on your right. As you near the coast stay close to the fence until you reach a broken gate. Go through the gate (ignore the direction arrows on the post) and follow the fence towards the sea keeping the fence on your right. You then have a steep descent (keep right) to the shore where you should head south round the headland and over a volcanic dyke. When you see the large patch of bushes under the cliff make your way up on the right hand side and you will find the cave half way up the cliff.

Meall a' Ghlamaidh (hill)

OS Grid Reference: 6324 4917

The location

Gigha's second highest hill reaches a height of 79m. It's remote location in Gigha's extreme west involves walking over some difficult terrain with an abundance of bracken and briars making it a challenge for the average walker. However, the views from the top make it worth the effort. The hill has been cultivated since medieval times with numerous traces of terraces, walls and enclosures. The highest part of the hill has evidence of extensive rig and furrow reflecting the way the land here was ploughed in past years. The best time to visit Meall a' Ghlamaidh is in spring.

Getting there

The easiest ascent of Meall a' Ghlamaidh is from the end of the path that leads to the Uamh nan Calaman cave (see page 14). From the top of the cliff above the cave walk uphill in a southerly direction keeping to the higher ground where heather grows to avoid extensive patches of bracken and briars. You can also approach the hill from Port an t-Samhlaidh and Ardlamey Farm via the old sheep fank on the lower slopes but this route is not recommended in summer due to the amount of bracken and briars which are present.

Above: Looking back to the summit of Meall a' Ghlamaidh on the right, with the bay and old stone jetty at Port an t-Samhlaidh on the left, and the Mull of Kintyre in the distance at far left.

Right: The east side of Meall a' Ghlamaidh overlooking Ardlamey has numerous crags and large fallen rocks.

Port na Gallochoille and beach

OS Grid Reference: 6544 4791

The location

The pretty port of Gallochoille, with its old stone jetty is still a working harbour used by small inshore boats. At low tide it is possible to walk over to Eilean a' Chùil and with a low spring tide you can across the sandy bay of Ceann an t-Sàilein back towards Ardminish. If you go around the headland at the far side of the jetty you will find a path which leads south to the pretty Gallochoille Beach. Behind the eastern end of the beach on a flat-topped rocky promontory lie the remains of Dùn Gallochoille fort. If you walk south from here along the shore you will reach another beach and an impressive volcanic dyke at Port an Sgiathain, 'Port of the Knife'.

Right: The lovely Gallochoille beach as seen from the path from the harbour. The Gaelic name "Gallochoille' possibly means 'Strangers Wood'.

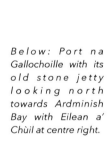

Below: Port na Gallochoille with its old stone jetty looking north towards Ardminish Bay with Eilean a' Chùil at centre right.

Getting there

Take the road south and soon after passing the sign for Achamore Gardens turn left and follow the track all the way to Gallochoille Cottages at the end of the track. Go through the small gate which leads to the harbour.

An Dòirlinn causeway

OS Grid Reference: 6585 4965

The location

It is best to undertake this walk at low tide. The route involves going through some rough terrain soon after the start. It is a lovely walk along the shore of Bàgh Druim Eòin with several islets to explore. The causeway at An Dòirlinn, 'isthmus', has been constructed with large rocks and links the two sections of the rugged Ardminish Point peninsula.

Getting there

Start from the entrance of the ferry car park and follow a small track to a bay of tidal flats. At the northern end of the bay look ahead for a single conifer tree on a small rocky outcrop (not the twin conifers) as a landmark. Head in that direction keeping to the left of the tree. The terrain here is difficult and no path exists. After a short distance you will reach Bàgh Druim Eòin. Walk round the bay on the right until you reach a stone dyke wall. Stay on the right of the wall and when you come to a gap go through to find the causeway close by. You can also reach the causeway by walking around the coast from the ferry car park entrance although some sections are rocky. When you reach the lovely sandy beach at Port Bàn head north through the vegetation on the top left of the beach and this will lead you directly to the causeway.

Above: View of the causeway looking south-east with the Kintyre peninsula in the distance.

Below: The causeway stretches across the gap between the two sections of land that make up the Ardminish Point peninsula. This is the view looking west towards Bàgh Druim Eòin.

Dùn Chibhich Iron Age fort

OS Grid Reference: 6450 5007

The location

Dùn Chibhich fort was likely a simple fortified structure used as a place of refuge for a family group. It would have been easy to defend due to its position on a steep sided rocky knoll at the end of a ridge. Its commanding position possibly made it the strongest fort on Gigha. The original entrance is on the south-east side and leads to a sunken court with the best preserved remains of the wall to the south. A possible outer court lies lower to the north-east. A rocky outcrop dominates the interior of the fort.

Getting there

Start at Gigha Golf Course and head uphill past the mast to access the field behind the farm. From the south west corner of the field curve round to the west until you reach the south end of a lochan. From here follow the marker poles and at the third pole take a right turn and follow a gully westwards until you reach a fourth pole. Here, head up the ridge and follow further poles towards the fort. From the final pole below the fort go straight towards the rocky outcrop and ascend by going left along a grassy ledge to the top.

Top: Dùn Chibhich overlooks Mill Loch.

Middle: The south wall and sunken interior court of the fort.

Bottom: The rocky knoll on which the fort sits as seen from the north

Port an Dùin watermill

OS Grid Reference: 6415 5065

The location

Port an Dùin watermill was constructed in the early 19th century at a time when the Ardailly area was an important and busy farming community. Much of the corn grown on Gigha would have been milled here and this particular mill specialised in producing oat-meal. The mill which is now a ruin and roofless is a T-shaped construction with a small attached building. Still intact is the impressive nearly 5m diameter cast iron waterwheel. It is of the more efficient 'overshot' design where water enters from the the top of the wheel. The mill's lade still flows from Mill Loch in the east. You should hear the water flowing in the lade as it runs right next to the track as you near the mill. The final section of the lade (now dry) is also cast iron. Large millstones can be found inside the building as well as part of the gearing for the wheel.

Getting there

Take the road north and at Druimyeon More Farm turn left onto a track and follow this all the way to the west coast. You will find the mill at the end of the road on your left.

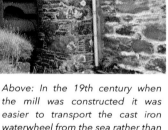

Above: In the 19th century when the mill was constructed it was easier to transport the cast iron waterwheel from the sea rather than overland.

Left: The interior of the mill with old millstones and gearing.

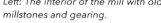

Above right: Looking down on Port an Dùin Mill from the mill lade. The cottage on the far side is private property.

Dùn an Trinnse fort

OS Grid Reference: 6421 5095

The location

Dùn an Trinnse, the 'Fort of the Trench', sits on the top of a steep sided rocky outcrop which overlooks Garbh Phort on Gigha's west coast. The entrance is through a gap on the west side. A natural gully on the north-east side of the knoll has been filled with rubble and faced with laid blocks to provide a secure base for the fort's wall. In the interior of the dun it is just possible to see the outline of a ruin of a rectangular building which partly overlies the dun wall. Just above the high water mark on the north side of the fort are three bait holes in the rocks. These are old cup-shaped rock carvings used for the preparation and holding of bait for fishing from the shore.

Getting there

Take the road north and follow the track on the left at Druimyeon More Farm towards Ardailly. When you pass the white farmhouse turn right and walk along the cattle track in a north-west direction to the shore at Garbh Port. Reach the fort by curving round its south side then ascending from the west.

Above: The view of the fort as you approach from Ardailly. The shore on the right is Garbh Phort. The Paps of Jura can be seen in the distance.

Above: The remains of the walls of Dùn an Trinnse are very clear to see from inside the fort. This is the view looking north.

Creag Bhàn (hill)

OS Grid Reference: 6478 5090

Location

'The white rock'. The hill is named after the rocks on its summit which have weathered to a pale colour. These rocks are around 635 million years old and were formed when the land that is now Gigha was in the southern hemisphere near the South Pole! The rocks have been rounded by ice moving in a south-west direction during the Late Devensian ice age which peaked 22,000 years ago. Creag Bhàn is the highest summit on Gigha and its 101 metres of height may seem diminutive, however the summit view surpasses that of many a Munro. You can see the whole island from here as well as many distant locations from Malin Head in the Republic of Ireland to Ben More on the Isle of Mull in the north, Ben Cruachan east of Oban and the Arran hills rising above Kintyre in the east.

Getting there

Take the north road and when you reach Druimyeon More Farm turn onto the Ardailly track on the left and follow it until just past the Mill Loch turn-off. Then turn right and head up the hill on a cattle track and hill path to the top. You will pass the Scottish Water holding reservoir en-route.

Above: Creag Bhàn as seen from the south. You can see the whole island from the summit.

Right: Spidean an Fhithitch, 'Raven's Pinnacle', marks the northern end of Creag Bhàn.

Right: The rocky summit has a useful view indicator.

Cnoc Largie (hill)

OS Grid Reference: 6568 5165

Above: The view north from close to the rocky summit of Cnoc Largie.

Bottom: Looking south from Cnoc Largie with Creag Bhàn on the far right.

The location

Cnoc Largie, also known as Highfield Hill is located close to the Ridh á Chailbeal burial ground. You will be able to look down on this important religious site from the summit. Your first view of Cnoc Largie is from the road - it is straight in front of you as you travel north from Ardminish. Although it is only 68m in height it is nevertheless a wonderful little hill, similar to Creag Bhàn, with a summit of smooth rocks and heather and wonderful views.

Getting there

Travelling on the road north take the track on the right a few hundred metres after Druimyeon More Farm. It is signposted to the Scottish Salmon Farm. Then immediately turn left and head up the field and through the gate on the left side. As you approach the top of the field look for a sheep path on the right leading through the bracken onto the ridge which itself leads to the summit. It is an easy walk and you will be rewarded with fine views.

Holy Stone

OS Grid Reference: 6541 5151

The location

Also known as the 'Fertility Stone', this impressive flat-topped stone was likely once used as a pagan altar and two cup marks are clearly visible on its south side. The three inscriptions on the stone are Early Christian and two depict elaborate Latin crosses although these are now very weathered and difficult to see. The Holy Stone was the place where childless women from the island undertook fertility rituals. The Holy Stone along with the Ridh' a' Chaibeal site and the Tobar a' Bheathaig well indicate that the Tarbert area of Gigha was a place of religious significance in the past.

Getting there

It can be difficult to locate but isn't far from the road. Between the Scottish Salmon turnoff and Tarbert Farm on the north road look for the second passing place on the left side of the road. Go through the field gate opposite on the right side of the road and follow the fence along the left edge of the field. When you reach the field corner go over into the rough ground and follow the wall on the left until you reach an area of boggy ground where you will find the stone on your right partially hidden by trees.

Above: The Holy Stone looking west towards Tarbert Farm.

Right: Twigs have been placed on the very worn inscriptions to mark their locations on the stone.

Below: Sketch of the Holy Stone inscriptions and cup marks.

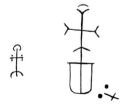

Ridh' a' Chaibeal – 'The Field of the Chapel'

OS Grid Reference: 6539 5161

The location

Ridh' a' Chaibeal, the 'Field of the Chapel', was once the religious centre of Gigha. In times past the site was a burial ground and it also had a chapel that predated the one at Kilchattan. A Celtic cross from this important religious site still remains standing but is badly damaged and weathered. Farmers in the past have cleared stones from the field, some of which would have been grave markers, and have moved them to this spot leaving a jumble of rocks. Unfortunately no trace of the chapel remains. Further down the field, just above the beach of Tràigh Bhàn an Tairbert is the location where a Viking bronze balance and weights were discovered. They had been placed in a stone box under a boulder and are now preserved in the Hunterian Museum in Glasgow.

Getting there

Take the road north and just before you reach Tarbert Farm look over to the field on your right. You will see a large collection of rocks lying in a bracken covered area surrounded by lush grass. This is what remains of Ridh' a' Chaibeal. Enter the field via the gate opposite the farm.

Right: The Celtic cross at Ridh' a' Chaibeal. The cross lies close to the Holy Stone (Pg 23) and and the Tobar a' Bheathaig well (Pg.25) indicating that this area was an important religious site in the past.

Right: These 10th century Viking bronze balance pans were discovered in 1849. They are similar to finds discovered in Viking graves in Norway.

Photo: University of Glasgow, Hunterian Museum.

Tobar a' Bheathaig - 'The well of the winds'

OS Grid Reference: 6564 5190

The location

St Beathag's Well is a shallow spring but better known on Gigha as the 'Great Well' and was said to have beneficial powers. It was deemed so important that it even had a guardian and anyone drinking the water would leave offerings. Some of these offerings can still be seen - quartz pebbles and pretty variegated stones. It gets its nickname from the fact that a person wishing a fair wind would visit and have the guardian throw water from the well in the direction that the wind was needed.

Getting there

The well can be difficult to locate although its position on the OS map is very accurate. Go past Tarbert Farm and take the track on the right into the field. Cross the field keeping the rough patch of high ground on the far side to your right. Cross the ditch (not easy) at the field boundary and look for boggy ground in the trees. Follow the stream-bed from the boggy area through the dense trees in a south east direction until you reach the spring.

The 'Well of the Winds' is a magical place at the foot of Cnoc Largie. It was tradition to keep the well capped when not in use for fear that its water would flood the island. In bygone days keepers of the well were appointed and their duties were passed down from mother to daughter

Kartli memorial

OS Grid Reference: 6537 5195

The location

On December 18 1991 a freak wave smashed into the Russian factory fishing ship Kartli resulting in the ship losing power and sending it onto a reef near the Isle of Gigha, killing four crew members. It was the last ship registered in the Soviet Union to be wrecked. A rescue was undertaken and forty-seven crew were saved thanks to the efforts of the Royal Air Force and Royal Navy, Islay lifeboat, the British tanker *Drupa* and local rescue services. The Kartli eventually grounded at Port Bàn near Slochd a' Chapuill on Gigha's west coast. Salvage operations were not undertaken due to the cost involved and the wreck disappeared under the waves during the winter of 1993. For the 25th anniversary of the accident, a memorial cairn with a specially commissioned bilingual plaque was unveiled. The memorial is located on Cnoc Eireachdais, the 'Hill of the Assembly', just a few metres past Tarbert Farm.

Getting there

Take the road north. When you reach Tarbert Farm look for the memorial cairn on a little hill adjacent to the road on your right.

Above: The ship's compass is embedded into the top of the cairn and the memorial plaque is attached to the side. The cairn overlooks West Tarbert Bay.

Carraigh an Tairbert standing stone

OS Grid Reference: 6555 5228

The location

Located at the narrowest part of the island, the very prominent 'Giant's Tooth' standing stone is one of the best known sights on Gigha. The two metre high stone sits on the grassy verge adjacent to the north road and possibly dates from the Bronze Age. It's not the oldest standing stone on Gigha. That honour goes to the one located near Kinererach further north although it is now just a stump. The 'Giant's Tooth' leans towards the east and has a natural cleft which over the years has weathered and divided the top into two points. The Scottish engineer Alexander Thom believed that the stone was a megalithic lunar observatory and others believe it was aligned with the Paps of Jura to mark the setting sun of the midsummer solstice.

Getting there

Go north past the shop passing both Druimyeon More Farm and then Tarbert Farm, the home of the Wee Isle Dairy. As you reach the narrowest part of the island between East and West Tarbert Bays you will find Carraigh an Tairbert on the right hand side of the road on the grassy verge.

Above: Also known as 'The Giant's Tooth', 'The Giant's Chip or Pebble', 'The Druid's Stone' and 'The Hanging Stone'. The latter name comes from from a tradition that people who were found guilty at nearby Cnoc Eireachdais, the 'Hill of the Assembly', had their heads positioned in the cleft of the stone and were then left to hang.

Eilean Garbh and the tombolo

OS Grid Reference: 6529 5412

The location

Eilean Garbh, 'Rough Isle', is a small island lying off the north west coast of Gigha. It is linked by a narrow stretch of sandy dunes called a tombolo formed by wind, waves and tidal currents. The tombolo is known as An Dòirlinn, meaning 'isthmus'. The north beach is named Queen's Beach after the visit in July 2006 by HM Queen Elizabeth II who visited Gigha aboard the *Hebridean Princess* for a holiday around the Scottish Islands to mark her 80th birthday. If you look closely on the south beach you might be lucky enough to find a tiny Gigha cowrie shell.   Eilean Garbh is rugged with rocky outcrops running along its spine. Be aware that it is barely accessible in the summer due to bracken and briars.

Getting there

Take the north road and at the Eilean Garbh footpath sign descend along what can be a very muddy track towards the tombolo.   At the fork in the path, left is less muddy but rougher while the right fork can be very muddy! Cross the tombolo to reach Eilean Garbh and follow the track which curves left. After a few metres take a sharp right and head up towards the rock face to a helpful ladder.

Right: The An Dòirlinn tombolo linking Gigha with Eilean Garbh. This view is looking back towards Gigha. The bay on the left is Bàgh na Dòirlinn and on the right is Bàgh Rubha Ruaidh.

Left: The rocky northern end of Eilean Garbh with Knapdale in the distance at far-right.

Below: A helpful ladder is in place to ascend the rock face on the lower slopes of Eilean Garbh.

Cnoc nan Gobhar (hill)

OS Grid Reference: 6613 5398

The location

Cnoc nan Gobhar is only 56m high but its location in the northern part of Gigha makes a visit to this little hill very worthwhile. As a viewpoint, it is one of the best on Gigha with Kintyre and the distant Arran hills to the east, Jura and Islay to the west and Knapdale to the north. If you turn south you look straight down the length of Gigha. It is also a good location to view Eilean Garbh and its tombolo. It would appear that a large 8m diameter cairn was once present on the summit but only a small one exists now. It is an easy ascent and the top has some large rounded rocks, similar, but on a smaller scale to those on Creag Bhàn. Care should be taken on the top of Cnoc nan Gobhar as the west side of the hill has a steep drop along its length.

Getting there

The starting point is the parking area next to the north road at the sign for 'Eilean Garbh'. Walk uphill immediately behind the parking area keeping the wall on your right. After a short distance veer left to the top of the hill. It has two tops, both with a cairn. The northern cairn is the highest point.

Above: The cairn on the summit of Cnoc nan Gobhar with Eilean Garbh and distant Islay in the background.

Above: The view looking south from Cnoc nan Gobhar down the spine of Gigha. In the distance, Cnoc Largie is on the left and Creag Bhàn at centre.

Fisherman's Cave

OS Grid Reference: 6611 5441

Above: The rocky shore is about 30m from the cave and the approach is via an indistinct path through nettles in the summer. Look out for the small wall and platform to the right of the entrance.

The location

The Fisherman's Cave is located on Gigha's north west shore on a raised beach in a nook of an old sea cliff. This cave has been well used over the years by Kintyre fisherman who not only lived in the cave but also used it for storing fishing equipment. It was likely abandoned in the early 20th century. It has a number of initials and dates carved into its northern wall, the earliest being 1735. Please do not add to these! Just outwith the entrance are a number of stone slabs possibly used for salting fish and also evidence of an old wall. Nearby, to the south west is a thirteen metre long causeway of stone blocks crossing a tidal channel linking the shore with a rocky island.

Getting there

At the northern end of the field opposite Cnoc nan Gobhar a path leads from the road to Port Cùil beach. From here follow the coast north for a few hundred metres. Go past the stone causeway and once around the rocky outcrops look inland to your right to spot a black and white marker pole. The cave is at the foot of the old cliff. You can also reach the cave from the northern beach at Eilean Garbh by walking along the rocky shore.

Above: Some of the ancient graffiti to be found in the cave. The earliest date to be found is 1735. Please do not add to the graffiti.

Càrn Bàn prehistoric cists

OS Grid Reference: 6681 5382

The location

'The White Cairn' is a neolithic chambered cairn, roughly circular with a diameter of around 15m which sits on a shelf of land some 9m above the sea at Port a' Chairn Bhàin. The cairn consists of four main cists and a number of smaller ones, although not all are visible. An old turf and stone wall would likely have surrounded the cairn. Much of the stone from the cairn was removed in the 18th century for wall building but a good spread of stones still exists. When first discovered a number of urns were found in the cists as well as human bones.

Getting there

Start at the end of the road in the north of the island and follow the yellow-topped marker poles along the coast in a south-east direction.   When you reach Port a' Chromain follow the marker poles on an indistinct path inland for approximately 250m. The cairn sits on the east side of the birch trees in an area which is overgrown with bracken and so the best time to visit is in spring. It is also possible to reach the site by following the rocky coast all the way round to Port a' Chairn Bhàin.

Above: Some of the central cists at Càrn Bàn

Right: Càrn Bàn is located in front of the prominent copse of birch trees seen here at upper left.

Càrn na Faire - 'Watch Cairn'

OS Grid Reference: 6626 5462

The location

The 'Watch Cairn' is located at the far north end of Gigha. It comprises a modern cairn sitting on top of a much older one. Much of the stone from the older cairn was removed in the 19th century and at that time it was reported that stones with markings and cup-marks were found and then returned to the cairn. It is possible that the original cairn formed part of a cist. In the past a large fire was lit on the top of the cairn to give the alarm to the neighbouring islanders of Islay & Jura when hostile parties were approaching. More recently it had a signal post to indicate when islanders wished the Islay steamer to pick up passengers from Gigha.

Getting there

Take the road north and at the road's highest point at the north end look for an old ruined building on your right where it is possible to park at the entrance of an old quarry. Walk north down the road and after 100m or so take the track on your left. You will see Càrn na Faire in the distance ahead. The route is marked with yellow-topped poles courtesy of Gigha Coast and Countryside Group.

Right: This view north-west clearly shows the modern cairn on top of the older 17m diameter cairn. The Paps of Jura are to the left. It is a wonderful viewpoint with Knapdale to the north, Islay and Jura to the west and Kintyre and the Arran hills to the east.

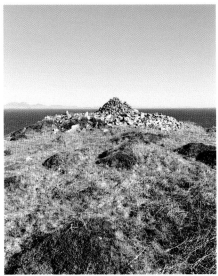

Above: This view from the cairn is looking north-east with Knapdale (left) and Kintyre (right) on the mainland in the distance.

Dark skies theatre

OS Grid Reference: 6650 5440

The location

Gigha is an island of beautiful countryside, white sandy beaches and wonderful coastal landscapes. When the Sun sets, another beautiful Gigha landscape appears - the night sky. Gigha has a stunning landscape of dark skies where our galaxy, the Milky Way, is clearly visible to the naked eye. Most of Gigha is free from light pollution but this is especially so at the far north of the island. An area between Port Righ (King's Bay) and Port Mòr has been designated as a dark skies theatre, with the 'production' being the beautiful night sky. It is a large flat grassy area above the stony beach and adjacent to the road end with 360° views of the sky and well away from any light pollution. It is an excellent spot to observe constellations, meteor showers, planets and other astronomical phenomena. The 'Northern Lights' can at times also be seen. The site is suitable to set up telescopes and cameras for a more detailed exploration of the night sky.

Getting there

Take the road north and go all the way to the end of the road between Port Righ and Port Mòr, the most northern part of the Isle of Gigha. Limited parking is available.

Above: The Milky Way seen in all its splendour from the Isle of Gigha.

Right: The Pleiades or 'Seven Sisters' open star cluster in the constellation Taurus.

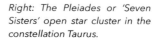

Further reading

Anderson, R.S.G., *The Antiquities of Gigha - A Survey and Guide*, 2nd Edition. The Galloway Gazette, 1978 (Reprint).

Czerkawska, Catherine, *The Way It Was - A History of Gigha*, Birlinn, 2016.

Dougan, Henry, *An Isle To Sail To - Gigha, The Faery Isle*, Self published, Glasgow, 1935.

Gigha Coast and Countryside Group, *Around and About - Isle of Gigha Walk Map*, Yellow Publications.

Gigha Path Network Group, *Walk Gigha*, Gigha, 2005.

Gillies, Freddy, *Life on God's island*, Northern Books from Famedram, 1999.

Gillies, Freddy, *The Magic of Gigha, Memories of 20th Century Life on God's Island*, Ardminish Press, 2006.

Lear, Helen, *The Essential Guide to the Isle of Gigha*, Gigha, 2007.

MacDonald, J.G., *Field Guide to the Geology of Gigha and Cara*, Geological Society of Glasgow, 2013.

Mercer, John, *Hebridean Islands - Colonsay Gigha Jura*, Blackie and Son, 1974.

Philip, K., *The Story of Gigha: The Flourishing Island*, Self published, Beith, Ayrshire, 1979.

Tulloch, Vie, *The Isle of Gigha, Wild Flowers, Birds and Mammals*, Ann Thomas Gallery, 1988.